RUBRICS
AND
MORE!

The **Assessment**, 2nd ed.
Companion

BERTIE KINGORE
AUTHOR

Jeffery Kingore
GRAPHIC DESIGN

PROFESSIONAL ASSOCIATES PUBLISHING

RUBRICS AND MORE!

The Assessment, 2nd ed. Companion

Grades Pre-K through 12

Copyright © 2002 Bertie Kingore

PUBLISHED BY
PROFESSIONAL ASSOCIATES PUBLISHING
PO Box 28056
Austin, Texas 78755-8056
PHONE/FAX: 512-335-1460

Printed in the United States of America
ISBN: 0-9657911-9-x

Table of Contents

Introduction

WHY <u>RUBRICS AND MORE?</u>

After the publication of <u>Assessment: Time-Saving Procedures for Busy Teachers</u> (Kingore, 1999), teachers and administrators asked for more adaptations and examples. The process worked for them and they wished to continue its value. They also asked for forms on a CD-ROM so they could customize assessment tools. This companion book is a response to those requests.

<u>Assessment: Time-Saving Procedures for Busy Teachers</u> (Kingore, 1999) is frequently referenced in this companion book. For simplification, it is referred to as <u>Assessment</u> instead of including the entire title.

<u>Rubrics and More!</u> and its accompanying CD-ROM provide several open-ended assessments, holistic rubrics, and analytical rubrics. This book greatly expands one of the most talked about features of the original book, the Rubric Generator. A new rubric process called the Developmental Rubric is also explained and several examples are included so teachers can begin communicating standards for quality as early as kindergarten. The Developmental Rubric can effectively incorporate district or state standards in instruction, and it communicates achievement growth over time.

Products Grid examples are also featured. Teachers commented that the original Products Grid helped them simplify differentiation and they needed more specific examples to facilitate applications. Five different Products Grids for specific subject areas and different ages of learners are included with lists of learning tasks that the products represent.

WHAT ARE RUBRICS?

Rubrics are guidelines to quality. They specify evaluation criteria and describe each value point on a scoring scale. Thus, a rubric is a scoring guide that describes the requirements for levels of proficiency as students respond to a learning task, open-ended question, or stated criteria. The purpose is to answer the question, "What are the conditions of quality, and to what degree has the student progressed toward that level of quality in the task?"

A rubric enables teachers to clarify to students what is expected in a learning experience and what to do in order to reach higher levels of achievement. To be effective, rubrics must be shared with students prior to beginning the task so they know the characteristics of quality work and have a clear target for which to aim.

WHO BENEFITS FROM RUBRICS?

Teachers benefit. Carefully constructed rubrics are relevant to instruction and guide teachers in designing lessons that enable students to reach higher levels of proficiency. Rubrics provide a standard for the grades in a grade book.

Kingore, B. (2002). <u>Rubrics and More!</u> Austin: Professional Associates Publishing.

Students benefit. Rubrics provide students with a clearer view of the merits and demerits of their work than grades alone communicate. Rubrics communicate to students that students are responsible for the grades they **earn** rather than to continue to view grades as something someone **gives** them.

Parents benefit. Rubrics more concretely explain to parents the student's levels of proficiencies and learning needs. Rubrics communicate more clearly the standard behind grades so parents understand why a child earns certain grades.

Thus, rubrics provide teachers, students, and parents with standards of excellence instead of relying on more subjective decisions. As Popham (1997) stated:

> *Rubrics represent not only scoring tools but also, more importantly, instructional illuminators.*

WHY USE RUBRICS?

One reoccurring difficulty in education is the subjective nature of assessment and evaluation. A rubric defuses this dilemma by providing a shared standard of quality. Rubrics are essential to help ensure consistency and fairness in evaluation, e.g., that different educators would assign similar grades to a work sample. Without a rubric, a grade of **A** may not mean the same thing in different classes.

The ongoing process of constructing effective rubrics invites professional conversations among grade-level teams and across grade levels. These conversations clarify instructional priorities. Together, educators determine the key attributes of learning tasks and discuss which criteria can be measured and taught. Thoughtfully developed rubrics make an important contribution to the quality of instruction.

Rubrics are standard in real-life situations. Increase parents', students' and other professionals' confidence in rubrics by reminding them of the large number of situations in which rubrics are consistently used.

> *Rubrics have been successfully used for years in the Olympics, Wall Street stock analysis, beauty contests, state and national level tests, and many professional competitions.*

Rubrics can be used for both goal setting and evaluation. First, provide a copy of a rubric and have students set goals before they begin the work by checking the levels they intend to achieve. Then, when the task is complete, the students use the same rubric copy for self-assessment with a second color of pen by marking their achievement level. Finally, teachers use the same rubric copy and a third color of pen to mark their evaluation of the achievement. Many teachers found that students' achievement increased when they used a rubric to goal set their intended level of success before they began the task. Setting their own target increases the students' determination to reach it.

Kingore, B. (2002). <u>Rubrics and More!</u> Austin: Professional Associates Publishing.

Open-Ended Assessment and Holistic Rubrics*

OPEN-ENDED ASSESSMENT FORMS

In order to effectively incorporate assessment and evaluation procedures in instruction, teachers need format samples to prompt their own development of procedures and assessment instruments. Open-ended formats with less writing are effective in primary through middle school classrooms to prompt students' reflections.

Two frequently requested open-ended assessment forms from the Assessment book are reproduced on the CD-ROM. Both the Discussion Assessment (shown to the right) and the Teamwork Assessment invite teachers to use the blank spaces to list the criteria specific to their group tasks. The same forms can be used more than once as different criteria can be listed when the tasks vary. Working as a group, students assess the quality of their work when the task is complete. The discussion that ensues is reflective and often encourages the refinement of group interaction skills for future group work. Examples of a completed Teamwork Assessment and a Discussion Assessment are found in Assessment, Chapter 9.

HOLISTIC RUBRICS

Holistic rubrics accent that all aspects of the work are related. All of the evaluative criteria are aggregated into a single qualitative score. The format of a holistic rubric is hierarchically arranged statements or paragraphs. Each level of proficiency describes the factors that would result in that level of quality. This evaluation is based on a consensus of the whole work and is useful when the objective is to focus on the demonstration or product as a whole.

Two holistic evaluation forms that teachers have particularly requested from the Assessment book are reproduced on the CD-ROM. With both the Editing Checklist Evaluation (shown to the right) and the Project Checklist Evaluation, the addition of a scoring scale to the descriptors and checklists allows a holistic conclusion to be reached about the quality of the work. The teacher,

Kingore, B. (2002). Rubrics and More! Austin: Professional Associates Publishing.

with input from class members if desired, lists statements on the numbered lines of the form that describe the task and designate the attributes of the task. When the learning task is complete, a student self-evaluates by filling out the checklist, finishing the sentence-stem reflections, and circling a holistic interpretation of the quality level attained. Then, the teacher uses the same copy of the form to complete an evaluation of the quality of the work.

Examples of a completed Editing Checklist Evaluation and a Project Checklist Evaluation can be found in Assessment, Chapter 9.

	Below Standard	Apprentice	Proficient	Exceeds Standards
Student's score:	D	C	B	A
Teacher's score:	D	C	B	A

Adapt the forms to match your grading needs by varying the scoring scale at the bottom of each form. Examples of possible variations are to the right to prompt your thinking.

	Novice	Developing	Adequately Developed	Fully Developed
Student's score:	1	2	3	4
Teacher's score:	1	2	3	4

	Unacceptable	Fair	Good	Excellent
Student's score:	Below 70	70-79	80-89	90-100
Teacher's score:	Below 70	70-79	80-89	90-100

The Open-Ended Product Evaluation forms on the next page are another example of holistic scoring. The first one is simple enough to be used by young learners. The second version is expanded in its descriptions of quality to communicate more clearly to older students. These forms are easily used by students to self-evaluate the merits of their products. The criteria at the top signal to students what is important as they begin work on their product. When the product is completed, students circle the score they earned. Teachers can also use a different color to evaluate on the same form if a grade in the grade book is desired. Furthermore, letter grades or percentages can be substituted for the scores of one through four as shown by the examples.

Another example of evaluation is shared in the form of a Product Evaluation that uses illustrations to communicate levels of quality to young learners or students with limited English reading skills. Teachers can fill in their preferred evaluation scale in the blanks at the bottom of the form.

With experience, students can be involved in developing their own versions of open-ended assessments and holistic evaluation instruments. Shifting students from consumers to producers increases their involvement and sense of ownership in assessment procedures. Using these forms as examples, encourage intermediate, middle school, and high school students to create their own open-ended assessment and evaluation forms. Enhance their enjoyment of the task by allowing them to incorporate illustrations and clever or humorous phrases.

*Refer to Chapter 9 of Assessment for a more complete discussion and additional examples of open-ended assessments and evaluations.

Kingore, B. (2002). Rubrics and More! Austin: Professional Associates Publishing.

OPEN-ENDED PRODUCT EVALUATION

EVALUATION CRITERIA:
Accuracy of information
Specificity of vocabulary
Depth of content
Complex level of information

SCORE

1
- Attempted a response
- Little evidence of content knowledge is present

2
- Limited information is provided
- Beginning-level vocabulary
- Limited but accurate content is incorporated

3
- Information is accurate
- Vocabulary is specific
- Response is supported with appropriate details
- Analysis is evident

4
- Provided more information than expected
- Vocabulary is advanced
- Response demonstrates a depth of content; meaningful
- Complex level of analysis and interpretation is reflected in the concepts or information

My product deserves this score because _____

OPEN-ENDED PRODUCT EVALUATION

EVALUATION CRITERIA:
Accurate information
Specific vocabulary
Content depth
Complex information

SCORE

1   I'm ready to learn more.

2   My product shows that I am beginning to understand.

3   My product has good content, vocabulary, and supporting ideas.

4   My product has lots of information, complex content, strong vocabulary, and I can explain it to others.

I scored myself this way because _____

Kingore, B. (2002). Rubrics and More! Austin: Professional Associates Publishing.

PRODUCT EVALUATION

1. Complete and detailed

2. Content and information

I wro	I wrote a little.	I wrote some. I learned.	I wrote interesting information. I tried to learn more.

3. Organization

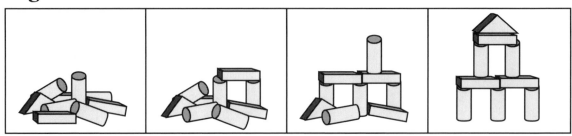

4. Neat and attractive

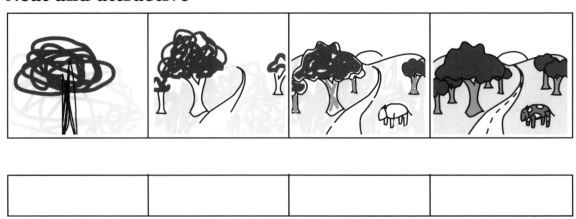

The Developmental Rubric

The Developmental Rubric is an example of a holistic rubric particularly effective with young learners. It takes the form of a poster in order to eliminate the need for paper copies and so that it can be placed where it is easily viewed by everyone in the classroom. A bonus value of the poster format is that anyone who visits the room can immediately identify the learning priorities of the class.

The rubric is developmental because it begins with one level of proficiencies and then increases the levels over time as skills develop. The use of faces and simple captions enhances visual appeal and enables the poster rubric to be read and understood by primary students. Rubrics for centers, behavior, and products are shared as examples of effective developmental rubric posters used in classrooms.

CONSTRUCTION PROCEDURES

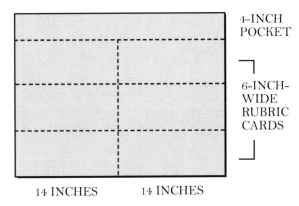

4-INCH POCKET

6-INCH-WIDE RUBRIC CARDS

14 INCHES   14 INCHES

MATERIALS:
- Two pieces of posterboard
- Copies of the faces and captions
- Crayons or markers.

Cut the first piece of the posterboard according to the dotted lines on the diagram to the right. These cuts result in one strip for the pocket of the poster and six cards. The six cards display the rubric proficiencies. Ascending skills or standards are written on each of the six cards to place in the poster when it is appropriate to express that level of challenge. One example of ascending skills on the rubric cards is shared on the next page for second grade writing standards.

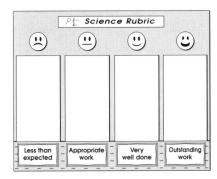

The second piece of posterboard is the foundation of your Pocket Chart Poster. Glue a title and faces onto the poster. Glue corresponding captions onto the separate strip for the pocket as the diagram to the left shows. Create your own captions or use the provided captions that focus on either effort or achievement. Staple the pocket strip onto the bottom of the poster to form places that hold the rubric cards.

Select captions that best communicate your instructional priorities. For example, some teachers prefer to emphasize the learning effort a child demonstrates at school. Other teachers want to accent the level of accomplishment a child experiences. One set of captions

Kingore, B. (2002). <u>Rubrics and More!</u> Austin: Professional Associates Publishing.

is included to address the effort a student expends when working. The second set ascribes the student's level of accomplishment. A blank form is also provided as a frame in which to copy and incorporate your own captions.

Use crayons or markers to color or outline the faces. Then, color each caption to match its corresponding face. These matching colors help clarify the evaluation levels to young learners. Finally, personalize your Pocket Chart Poster with additional color and designs.

CORRELATING TO STATE OR DISTRICT STANDARDS

Incorporate state standards into this rubric format so young students and other observers have a clear idea of the learning targets to be achieved over time. Initially, refer to your state or district standards to determine the desired level and kinds of skills in one curriculum area for the beginning of the school year. List those outcomes on one card to place in the highest proficiency level on the rubric chart. Card number four on the second grade writing example that follows displays that level. Next, determine the descending levels of skills that lead to the proficiencies on card four. Those skill levels are listed on cards one, two, and three.

Second Grade Writing--Beginning of the Year

I did not try.	I tried to write neatly.	My writing is neat.	I wrote carefully and used good spacing.	My writing is carefully formed.	My writing is very readable.
	I used capitals and lower-case letters in my sentences.	I wrote more than one sentence.	I wrote several interesting sentences.	I wrote descriptive sentences.	My writing communicates well.
	I wrote my name and the date.	I sounded out and spelled most of the words I used.	I spelled sight words correctly.	I wrote a beginning, middle, and end.	I wrote complete and elaborated sentences and paragraphs.
				I sounded out the words and checked my spelling.	I checked my capitalization, spelling, and punctuation.
Card 1	Card 2	Card 3	Card 4	Card 5	Card 6

Cards five and six list the levels of skill proficiencies to be developed next. When students are proficient at level four, the teacher reorders the cards. Level one might remain the same if the teacher wants to make it clear that not trying is the main reason for not achieving in the class. Card two is removed; card three moves into the second position, card four moves into the third position, and card five is added as the new proficiency goal in the fourth position. Later, as skills accelerate, the card levels shift again and card six is placed in the rubric poster. Continue the process throughout the year by developing additional cards as skills reach new levels.

Kingore, B. (2002). <u>Rubrics and More!</u> Austin: Professional Associates Publishing.

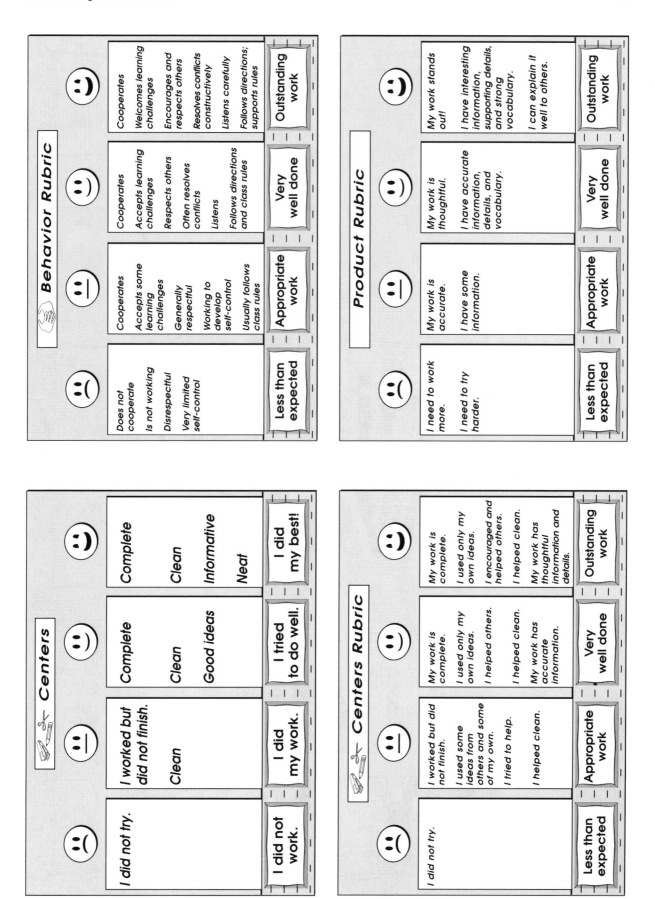

Behavior Rubric

Outstanding work 😊
- Cooperates
- Welcomes learning challenges
- Encourages and respects others
- Resolves conflicts constructively
- Listens carefully
- Follows directions; supports rules

Very well done 🙂
- Cooperates
- Accepts learning challenges
- Respects others
- Often resolves conflicts
- Listens
- Follows directions and class rules

Appropriate work 😐
- Cooperates
- Accepts some learning challenges
- Generally respectful
- Working to develop self-control
- Usually follows class rules

Less than expected ☹️
- Does not cooperate
- Is not working
- Disrespectful
- Very limited self-control

Product Rubric

Outstanding work 😊
- My work stands out!
- I have interesting information, supporting details, and strong vocabulary.
- I can explain it well to others.

Very well done 🙂
- My work is thoughtful.
- I have accurate information, details, and vocabulary.

Appropriate work 😐
- My work is accurate.
- I have some information.

Less than expected ☹️
- I need to work more.
- I need to try harder.

✂️ Centers

I did my best! 😊
- Complete
- Clean
- Informative
- Neat

I tried to do well. 🙂
- Complete
- Clean
- Good ideas

I did my work. 😐
- I worked but did not finish.
- Clean

I did not work. ☹️
- I did not try.

✂️ Centers Rubric

Outstanding work 😊
- My work is complete.
- I used only my own ideas.
- I encouraged and helped others.
- I helped clean.
- My work has thoughtful information and details.

Very well done 🙂
- My work is complete.
- I used only my own ideas.
- I helped others.
- I helped clean.
- My work has accurate information.

Appropriate work 😐
- I worked but did not finish.
- I used some ideas from others and some of my own.
- I tried to help.
- I helped clean.

Less than expected ☹️
- I did not try.

Kingore, B. (2002). <u>Rubrics and More!</u> Austin: Professional Associates Publishing.

Effort Caption 1

I did not work.

Effort Caption 2

I did my work.

Effort Caption 3

I tried to do well.

Effort Caption 4

I did my best!

Accomplishment Caption 1

Less than expected

Accomplishment Caption 2

Appropriate work

Accomplishment Caption 3

Very well done

Accomplishment Caption 4

Outstanding work

1.

2.

Behavior

© 2002 Bertie Kingore

Kingore, B. (2002). <u>Rubrics and More!</u> Austin: Professional Associates Publishing.

3.

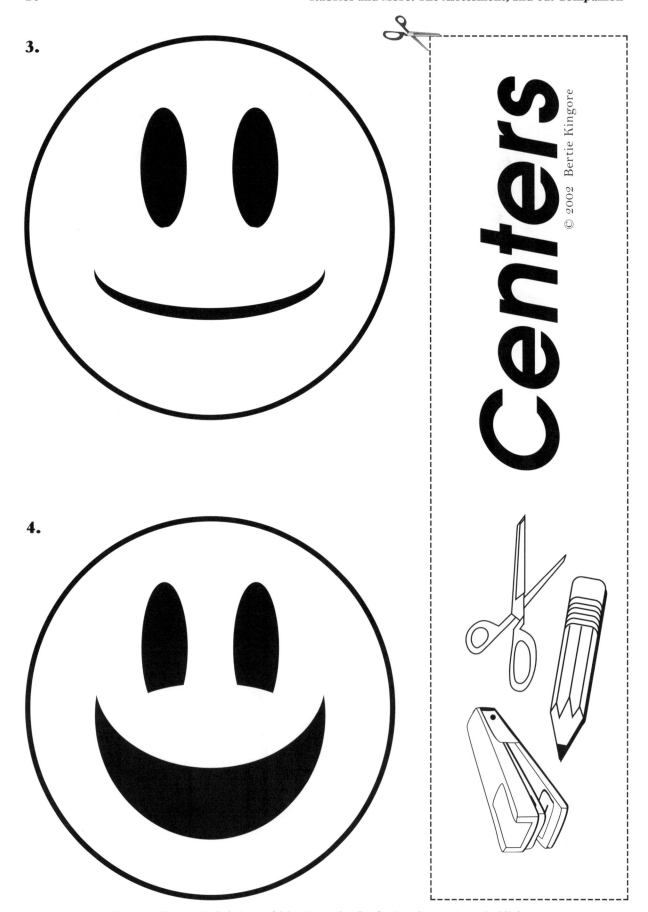

4.

Centers

© 2002 Bertie Kingore

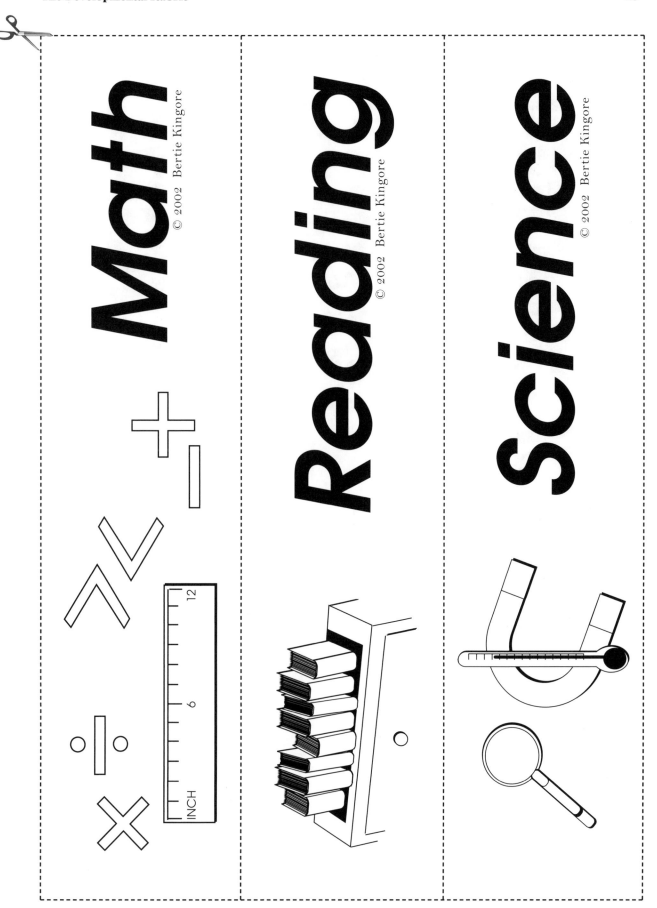

Kingore, B. (2002). <u>Rubrics and More!</u> Austin: Professional Associates Publishing.

Social Studies

© 2002 Bertie Kingore

Writing

© 2002 Bertie Kingore

Rubric

TAB A

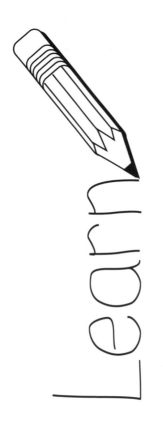

If you want to add the word "Rubric" onto the title of your rubric poster, glue **Tab A** to the back of the right end of the subject area title you are using. If you do not plan to use a subject area title, the Rubric caption can serve as the complete title.

The Rubric Generator*

The Rubric Generator is a device I developed to enable teachers to more easily create analytical rubrics for any learning task. An analytical rubric is a list of task-specific criteria with varying levels of success listed separately beside each criterion. This evaluation form allows the separate analysis of each criterion instead of analyzing the product as a whole. Thus, analytical rubrics enable teachers and students to recognize that students' degrees of proficiency may vary among the different criteria of the work. For example, a student might score very high in task commitment but slightly lower in complexity.

The Rubric Generator presented here is a revised and expanded version of the original work published in <u>Assessment</u>. Four additional pages of criteria have been added to facilitate rubric development. This Rubric Generator may prove useful for your evaluation needs or serve as a model for developing your own rubric generator.

In this section, the Rubric Generator is first presented with expanded descriptors to more specifically communicate what constitutes quality work. This version is most useful when communicating with adults, mature students, or when detailed rubrics are needed. The Rubric Generator is then presented in a simplified version. This version is useful when brief rubrics are needed or when more simple rubrics would communicate clearly to a specific student population.

USING THE RUBRIC GENERATOR

The Rubric Generator enables teachers to create rubrics in less time and with less frustration by duplicating, cutting, and pasting components instead of starting from scratch each time. The process allows teachers to customize rubrics for contents, products, and processes. The following is a general sequence for creating a rubric from the Rubric Generator.

1. SELECT APPLICABLE CRITERIA.--Skim the Rubric Generator and any rubrics you have developed to determine the specific criteria crucial to your intended assignment.

2. COPY CRITERIA STRIPS.--Photocopy the applicable criteria and levels of proficiencies.

3. ORGANIZE THE CRITERIA.--Place those criteria strips on the blank rubric page shared in this section.

4. REVIEW AND REWRITE THE STRIPS.--As you plan a specific learning experience for your students, rewrite and adapt the criteria strips. Add to them and rewrite any descriptors for which you have a better idea.

Kingore, B. (2002). <u>Rubrics and More!</u> Austin: Professional Associates Publishing.

Consider the following as you generate your rubric.

*   How many and which criteria best describe the product? Experienced teachers recommend a thoughtful focus on only the most significant criteria. They suggest limiting the rubric to one page whenever possible.
*   Reword the levels for each criterion as needed to communicate your decisions about quality work and match the readiness level of your students.
*   Use points, percentages, or grades to weight each criterion. Weighting designates the relative importance of each criterion so students understand where to focus their learning time and effort.
*   Have other educators read your rubric to offer suggestions.
*   If feasible, try the rubric in more than one class. Rewrite specific word choices based on those results.
*   When appropriate, elicit ideas for clarification and change from students.

STUDENT-DEVELOPED RUBRICS

After students have experience using rubrics, involve them in rewriting a rubric from the expanded descriptors. The objectives are:
1. To increase students' ownership in the task;
2. To increase students involvement in interpreting the levels of proficiency on a rubric; and
3. To make the rubric more directly applicable to a specific learning assignment.

The following procedure has been successfully implemented in many classrooms and typically takes twenty to twenty-five minutes of class time to complete.
1. The teacher pre-selects five to seven criteria strips from the rubric generator that are applicable to the intended learning experience.
2. The teacher hands out copies of the selected criteria strips to the class and involves them in determining which four to six criteria they think are most important for the assignment. At times, the teacher may designate that one or two of the criteria are required. For example, a teacher may announce that content depth is vital to the assignment and must be one of the final five criteria.
3. The class is then divided into groups and each group is given one criterion strip to evaluate and rewrite for five minutes. To facilitate class sharing, give each group a strip of an overhead transparency on which to copy their final criterion strip.
4. The rewritten strips are placed on the overhead to facilitate review by the whole class. Additional suggestions and responses are considered before the final copy is adopted.
5. The edited criteria strips are then photocopied and distributed to the class as the task rubric when the assignment begins.

*Refer to Chapter 10 of <u>Assessment</u> for a more complete discussion of analytical rubrics and examples of rubrics constructed from the Rubric Generator. Chapter 10 also offers additional suggestions to involve students in using the rubric generator to construct class rubrics.

Kingore, B. (2002). <u>Rubrics and More!</u> Austin: Professional Associates Publishing.

RUBRIC

	Below Standard	Apprentice	Proficient	Exceeds Standards
Appearance Points 18/20	Inadequate; not neat; little care evident below 14	Adequate; needs more careful work and attention to detail 14-15	Attractive and visually appealing; neatly completed 16-17	Eye catching; aesthetically pleasing; beyond expectations (18) 20
Carried out plan Points 8/10	Did not complete plan or lacked plan below 7	Completed with frequent assistance and prompting 7	Completed plan; limited prompting needed (8)	Followed through well; autonomous; exceeded expectations 9-10
Complexity Points 34/40	Insufficient or irrelevant information below 28	Simple and basic information; limited critical thinking is evident 28-31	Critical thinking evident; compares and contrasts; integrates topics, time, or disciplines (32-35)	Beyond expected level; analyzes multiple perspectives and issues; abstract thinking 36-40
Time management Points 8/10	Did not complete task	Needed frequent assistance	Used time appropriately (8)	Autonomous; mature time management 9-10
Written reflection Points 14/20	Lacks content understanding; no effort evident below 14	Content reflects a beginning level of understanding; tried to address the topic (14-15)	Addresses major content points; some interpretation; appropriate effect 16-17	Clearly interprets and synthesizes content; high-level response and effort 18-20

Total Grade Points
82/100

B-

COMMENTS

Jamie, I am very pleased with your critical thinking and the total appearance of your project. You tried hard to present more complex information and you succeeded. Your written reflections need more depth, however. Consider rewriting it and re-evaluating your total project.

Adapted from: Kingore, B. (1999). Assessment. 2nd ed. Austin: Professional Associates Publishing.

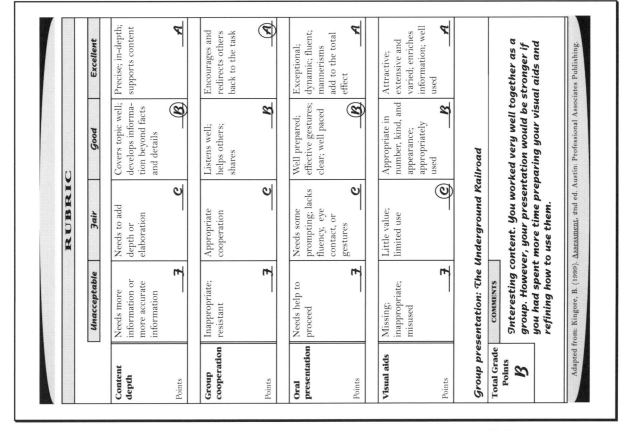

RUBRIC

	Unacceptable	Fair	Good	Excellent
Content depth Points	Needs more information or more accurate information F	Needs to add depth or elaboration C	Covers topic well; develops information beyond facts and details (B)	Precise; in-depth; supports content A
Group cooperation Points	Inappropriate; resistant F	Appropriate cooperation C	Listens well; helps others; shares B	Encourages and redirects others back to the task (A)
Oral presentation Points	Needs help to proceed F	Needs some prompting; lacks fluency, eye contact, or gestures C	Well prepared; effective gestures; clear; well paced (B)	Exceptional; dynamic; fluent; mannerisms add to the total effect A
Visual aids Points	Missing; inappropriate; misused F	Little value; limited use (C)	Appropriate in number, kind, and appearance; appropriately used B	Attractive; extensive and varied; enriches information; well used A

Total Grade Points
B

COMMENTS

Group presentation: The Underground Railroad

Interesting content. You worked very well together as a group. However, your presentation would be stronger if you had spent more time preparing your visual aids and refining how to use them.

Adapted from: Kingore, B. (1999). Assessment. 2nd ed. Austin: Professional Associates Publishing.

RUBRIC

Adapted from: Kingore, B. (1999). Assessment, 2nd ed. Austin: Professional Associates Publishing.

Kingore, B. (2002). Rubrics and More! Austin: Professional Associates Publishing.

RUBRIC GENERATOR: Expanded Descriptors

Appearance	Inadequate; not neat; little care evident	Adequate; needs more careful work and attention to detail	Attractive and visually appealing; neatly completed	Eye catching; aesthetically pleasing; beyond expectations
Points /	_____	_____	_____	_____

Application	Attempts task with limited skill	Hesitant to proceed independently; errors are present	Correct response or solution with minimal prompting or errors	Skillful application; higher-level response than expected
Points /	_____	_____	_____	_____

Carried out plan	Did not complete plan or lacked plan	Completed with frequent assistance and prompting	Completed plan; limited prompting needed	Followed through well; autonomous; exceeded expectations
Points /	_____	_____	_____	_____

Communi-cation	Not able to discuss; confused or disjointed	Needs prompting to explain or discuss; lacks a clear focus	Adequate explanation or discussion; appropriate vocabulary	Explains independently, clearly, and confidently; precise vocabulary
Points /	_____	_____	_____	_____

Complexity	Insufficient or irrelevant information	Simple and basic information; limited critical thinking is evident	Critical thinking evident; compares and contrasts; integrates topics, time, or disciplines	Beyond expected level; analyzes multiple perspectives and issues; abstract thinking
Points /	_____	_____	_____	_____

Kingore, B. (2002). Rubrics and More! Austin: Professional Associates Publishing.

RUBRIC GENERATOR: Expanded Descriptors

Compre-hension Points /	No comprehension is demonstrated _____	Response reflects a beginning level of understanding _____	Appropriate use of details and vocabulary; adequate understanding _____	Precise vocabulary; supportive ideas; related concepts; demonstrates thorough under-standing _____

Constructs meaning Points /	Needs clarity and focus; undeveloped _____	Attempts to construct meaning but rambles; unclear _____	Information is generally clear and understandable _____	Cohesive; meaningful; clearly focused; precise; in-depth analysis _____

Content depth Points /	Needs more information or more accurate information _____	Valid content but little depth or elaboration; sparse _____	Covers topic effectively; well developed; explores the topic beyond facts and details _____	Precise data; in-depth; well sup-ported; develops complex concepts and relationships _____

Creativity Points /	Used others ideas or responses _____	Typical or clichéd responses; little original thinking _____	Creative integration; enhances more typical ideas or responses _____	Unique ideas or responses; insightful; fresh perspective; novel; imaginative _____

Discussion Points /	No verbal or nonverbal participation demonstrated _____	Some participation with prompting _____	Nonverbally interacts; appro-priate verbal participation _____	Nonverbally encourages others; verbal responses reflect analysis and active learning _____

Kingore, B. (2002). <u>Rubrics and More!</u> Austin: Professional Associates Publishing.

RUBRIC GENERATOR: Expanded Descriptors

✂ -

Effort/task commitment	Apathetic; resistant	Incomplete or inadequate for task	Appropriate effort; successful	Extensive commitment; rigorous effort; autonomous
Points /	_____	_____	_____	_____

- -

Fluency	Short, choppy, or incomplete sentences	Generally complete, simple sentences; some run-on sentences	Well-constructed and varied sentences; smooth transitions	Crafted with a variety in sentence length and structure that enhances the total effect; fluid
Points /	_____	_____	_____	_____

- -

Group cooperation	Inappropriate; resistant	Appropriate effort and cooperation	Listens attentively; helps others; shares appropriately	Encourages and redirects others back to task; negotiates; resolves conflict
Points /	_____	_____	_____	_____

- -

Idea development	No clear focus or main idea; details are confusing	Stated main idea; most details relate to it	Clear focus; appropriate main idea; details relate and clarify ideas	Cohesive; well defined and elaborated main idea; details increase interest and meaning
Points /	_____	_____	_____	_____

- -

Integration of skills	Unable to apply skills; weak	Attempts to integrate information and skills in only one subject area	Demonstrates skill mastery by applying skills in multiple subject areas	Consistently integrates information and skills in process and product; skillful
Points /	_____	_____	_____	_____

Kingore, B. (2002). Rubrics and More! Austin: Professional Associates Publishing.

RUBRIC GENERATOR: Expanded Descriptors

Knowledge of the text Points /	Little knowledge evident; lacks key ideas ___	Limited familiarity of textual concepts or key ideas ___	Understands most major ideas and concepts; uses some appropriate text references ___	In-depth knowledge of concepts and relationships; supports with references relevant to text ___

Oral presentation Points /	Needs prompting and assistance ___	Addressed topic; needed prompting; lacked fluency, eye contact, or gestures ___	Well prepared; clear; well paced generally effective speaking techniques ___	Exceptional; dynamic; fluent; speech and mannerisms enhance communication ___

Organization Points /	Unclear; lacks organization ___	Attempts to organize and sequence but is hard to follow ___	Organized effectively; a clear sequence; well structured ___	Coherent; skillfully planned; logically sequenced and organized to communicate well ___

Personal connection Points /	Lacking, insufficient, or irrelevant ___	Limited attempt to relate topic to self ___	Credible connection made between learner and topic; analysis is evident ___	Fully supported and cohesive connection; complex analysis demonstrated ___

Problem interpretation Points /	Misunderstands the problem ___	Basically understands the problem; flaws in interpretation ___	Generally correct interpretation and explanation; appropriate response ___	Well analyzed and explained interpretation; clearly understands problem ___

Kingore, B. (2002). <u>Rubrics and More!</u> Austin: Professional Associates Publishing.

RUBRIC GENERATOR: Expanded Descriptors

✂ -

Problem solving Points /	Inappropriate process or solution ____	Incomplete or limited in application; logic is flawed ____	Appropriate process and application; analytical thinking is evident ____	High-level solution; innovative; synthesizes; evaluates ____

- -

Resources Points /	Inappropriate, unrelated, or no sources used for documentation ____	Minimal resources used appropriately ____	Appropriate in quantity, quality, and application ____	Extensive, varied, and appropriate; high caliber; incorporates advanced technology ____

- -

Strategies Points /	Inappropriate	Limited application; not sure of process; incomplete or flawed ____	Successfully applies a limited number of strategies; appropriate process ____	Advanced strategies are independently implemented; flexible and innovative ____

- -

Time management Points /	Did not complete task	Needed frequent assistance ____	Used time appropriately ____	Autonomous; mature time management ____

- -

Visual aids Points /	Incomplete or inappropriate; misused ____	Ineffective; minimal visuals; limited application ____	Appropriate in quantity, quality, and appearance; appropriately used to support information ____	High visual appeal; extensive and varied; enhances and integrates information; skillfully used ____

Kingore, B. (2002). <u>Rubrics and More!</u> Austin: Professional Associates Publishing.

RUBRIC GENERATOR: Expanded Descriptors

✂ -

Vocabulary	Some words are inappropriate or used incorrectly	Words and phrases are simple or vague	Descriptive and interesting language is used appropriately with elaboration	Uses specific terminology; precise, advanced language; rich imagery
Points /	_____	_____	_____	_____

- -

Writing conventions • Grammar • Punctuation • Spelling • Capitalization • Paragraphing Points /	Serious errors makes reading and understanding difficult	Frequent errors present but content is readable; emerging skills	Minimal errors; mechanics and spelling are typical and appropriate for grade level	The product is enhanced by the skillful application of mechanics; fluid
	_____	_____	_____	_____

- -

Written reflection	Lacks content understanding; no effort evident	Content reflects a beginning level of understanding; tried to address the topic	Addresses major content points; some interpretation; appropriate effect	Clearly interprets and synthesizes content; high-level response and effort
Points /	_____	_____	_____	_____

- -

Points /	_____	_____	_____	_____

- -

Total Grade Points /	**COMMENTS**

Kingore, B. (2002). <u>Rubrics and More!</u> Austin: Professional Associates Publishing.

RUBRIC GENERATOR: Simple Descriptors

✂ --

Appearance Points /	Inadequate; not neat _____	Needs more attention to detail _____	Attractive; neat _____	Eye catching; beyond expectations _____

Application Points /	Limited attempt _____	Not able to proceed independently; errors _____	Correct response; little prompting; few if any errors _____	High-level response; skillful _____

Carried out plan Points /	Lacked a plan; not complete _____	Completed with frequent assistance _____	Completed with little help _____	Followed through well; self-motivated _____

Communi-cation Points /	Does not discuss _____	Needs prompting and focus _____	Adequately explains or discusses _____	Clear and confident; uses strong vocabulary _____

Complexity Points /	Too simple or not appropriate _____	Simple information; limited critical thinking _____	Information shows critical thinking; compares and contrasts _____	Beyond expected level; analyzes from multiple points of view _____

Kingore, B. (2002). _Rubrics and More!_ Austin: Professional Associates Publishing.

RUBRIC GENERATOR: Simple Descriptors

✂ -

Compre-hension Points /	Does not comprehend _____	Beginning level of understanding _____	Adequate understanding; appropriate details _____	Thorough under-standing; precise vocabulary, details, and concepts _____

- -

Constructs meaning Points /	Undeveloped _____	Unclear; rambles _____	Clear and understandable _____	Meaningful; clear focus; precise _____

- -

Content depth Points /	Needs more information or more accurate information _____	Needs to add depth or elaboration _____	Covers topic well; develops informa-tion beyond facts and details _____	Precise; in-depth; supports content _____

- -

Creativity Points /	Used others ideas _____	Typical responses; little creativity _____	Creative; added to more typical ideas _____	Unique ideas or responses; novel; fresh _____

- -

Discussion Points /	Does not participate _____	Needed prompting _____	Appropriate nonverbal and verbal interaction _____	Verbally and nonverbally demonstrates analysis and active listening _____

Kingore, B. (2002). <u>Rubrics and More!</u> Austin: Professional Associates Publishing.

RUBRIC GENERATOR: Simple Descriptors

- -

Effort/task commitment Points /	Resistant _____	Inadequate for task _____	Appropriate effort and time on task _____	Extensive effort; uses time well; self-motivated _____

Fluency Points /	Choppy; incomplete _____	Simple sentences; some run-on sentences _____	Varied, well-constructed sentences _____	Sentences vary in length and structure; fluid _____

Group cooperation Points /	Inappropriate; resistant _____	Appropriate cooperation _____	Listens well; helps others; shares _____	Encourages and redirects others back to the task _____

Idea development Points /	Simple; not clear; confusing _____	States a main idea; most details fit _____	Appropriate main idea and details; clear _____	Well developed main idea with meaningful details _____

Integration of skills Points /	Unable to apply skills _____	Uses information and skills in only one subject area _____	Accurately applies skills in multiple subject areas _____	Consistently integrates skills and information; skillful _____

Kingore, B. (2002). <u>Rubrics and More!</u> Austin: Professional Associates Publishing.

RUBRIC GENERATOR: Simple Descriptors

✂---

Knowledge of the text	Little knowledge	Limited concepts and ideas	Understands most key ideas and concepts	In-depth knowledge; uses text to support ideas
Points /	_____	_____	_____	_____

Oral presentation	Needs help to proceed	Needs some prompting; lacks fluency, eye contact, or gestures	Well prepared; effective gestures; clear; well paced	Exceptional; dynamic; fluent; mannerisms add to the total effect
Points /	_____	_____	_____	_____

Organization	Unorganized	Hard to follow	Effectively structured; a clear sequence	Skillfully planned; clearly organized and sequenced; logical
Points /	_____	_____	_____	_____

Personal connection	Lacking	Limited	Relates topic to self; analyzes	Clearly explains and supports connection between self and topic
Points /	_____	_____	_____	_____

Problem interpretation	Misunderstands	Only a basic understanding	Generally correct interpretation; appropriate explanation	Well analyzed interpretation; clearly understands
Points /	_____	_____	_____	_____

Kingore, B. (2002). Rubrics and More! Austin: Professional Associates Publishing.

RUBRIC GENERATOR: Simple Descriptors

✂ -

Problem solving	Inappropriate	Incomplete or flawed	Appropriate process and application; effective analysis	High-level solution; innovative; synthesizes; evaluates
Points /	_____	_____	_____	_____

Resources	Inappropriate	A few resources used appropriately	Appropriate in number, kind, and use	Extensive and varied; uses technology
Points /	_____	_____	_____	_____

Strategies	Inappropriate	Incomplete or flawed application	Uses limited strategies but applies them appropriately	Effective use of advanced strategies; flexible
Points /	_____	_____	_____	_____

Time management	Did not complete task	Needed frequent assistance	Used time appropriately	Mature management
Points /	_____	_____	_____	_____

Visual aids	Missing; inappropriate; misused	Little value; limited use	Appropriate in number, kind, and appearance; appropriately used	Attractive; extensive and varied; enriches information; well used
Points /	_____	_____	_____	_____

Kingore, B. (2002). <u>Rubrics and More!</u> Austin: Professional Associates Publishing.

RUBRIC GENERATOR: Simple Descriptors

✂ -

Vocabulary Points /	Words are used incorrectly _____	Simple words and phrases _____	Descriptive; interesting; uses elaboration _____	Advanced; uses specific terms; rich imagery _____

- -

Writing conventions • Grammar • Punctuation • Spelling • Capitalization • Paragraphing Points /	Serious errors make it hard to understand _____	Frequent errors but readable; emerging skills _____	Few errors; appropriate for grade level _____	Skillful application of mechanics _____

- -

Written reflection Points /	Lacks content and effort _____	Beginning content level; tried _____	Appropriate content and effort; some interpretation _____	High-level response and effort; clear interpretation _____

- -

    Points /	 _____	 _____	 _____	 _____

- -

Total Grade Points /	**COMMENTS**

Kingore, B. (2002). <u>Rubrics and More!</u> Austin: Professional Associates Publishing.

The Products Grid*

The original Products Grid in <u>Assessment</u> organizes over 110 potential products for learning tasks. Students vary so dramatically in their strengths, needs, and best ways to learn that the differences are boggling in most classrooms. Teachers compliment the Products Grid as one tool that helps them differentiate learning experiences and products to assign. Each product is listed in alphabetical order for quick reference and is coded to the modalities and intelligences the student primarily uses to complete the product and present or share it with others.

In addition to matching the best ways for students to learn, the objective of a products grid is to replace simple, right-answer sheets that require little thinking with tasks that encourage active participation and challenge students to generate responses. To advance learning, the products must connect to content and invite students to apply and transfer acquired skills. The intent is not to entertain students but rather to engage them so appropriately in learning experiences that enjoyment results. Experienced teachers report that these products also serve as springboards for increased discussion and interaction among students.

Modality codes		
V	=	visual;
O/A	=	oral/auditory;
W	=	written; and
K	=	kinesthetic

Multiple Intelligence codes		
L	=	linguistic;
L-M	=	logical-mathematical;
N	=	naturalist;
S	=	spatial;
M	=	musical;
B-K	=	bodily kinesthetic;
Inter	=	interpersonal; and
Intra	=	intrapersonal.

Teachers frequently ask for products grids more specifically related to one subject area and/or grade level. For example, which math products might increase critical thinking responses and help balance the use of skill sheets? In response to those requests, five specific products grids follow. These grids are customized for limited readers and writers, primary students, and the subject areas of language arts and social studies, math, and science.

Most products are self-explanatory, however, some merit examples for clarification. While many different content-related tasks are possible, some suggestions for the less obvious products are offered to prompt your thinking of applications useful in your instruction.

A Product Grid Form

A blank form for a products grid is provided on the CD-ROM so you can organize your own instructional product choices. Alphabetically list the products most applicable to your teaching and then code each product to the learning modalities and multiple intelligences primarily used by students to produce and present that product.

*Refer to Chapter 11 of <u>Assessment</u> for a more complete discussion of the Products Grid and its multiple possibilities for instructional applications.

Kingore, B. (2002). <u>Rubrics and More!</u> Austin: Professional Associates Publishing.

Product Examples for Learners with Limited Reading and Writing Skills

- ACROSTIC--Use a concept or topic word such as *families.* Students brainstorm ideas as an adult writes significant words or phrases related to the topic that begin with each letter in the word.

- ALPHABET CHART FOR A TOPIC--For each letter of the alphabet, brainstorm and list to organize important facts and ideas about a topic.

- AUDIO TAPE--Record students retelling a folk tale or well-known story at the beginning, middle, and end of the year to hear and celebrate skills and growth in story structure, vocabulary, and language fluency.

- CHORAL READING/READERS THEATER--Divide well-known poems or rhymes into parts for children to perform.

- COLLECTION COLLAGE--Make a collage of items found in even numbers or items of a certain color, textures, or size.

- DANCE--Create a dance to show how certain animals move.

- DEMONSTRATION--Demonstrate a simple sequence or task, such as how to get to school when it is raining.

- DIORAMA--Make a diorama illustrating a problem or solution in a story the class is reading.

- FLANNEL BOARD PRESENTATION--Glue small velcro or sandpaper pieces to paper illustrations and place them on a flannel board as you retell a story or sequence.

- GRAPH--Graph how many classmates are: 1. eating turkey on Thanksgiving or eating something else; 2. having company at their house during the holidays or not having company; 3. getting to school by walking, car, bus, bike, or another way.

- INTERVIEW--1. Tape record interviews with other students. 2. Interview family members to learn about family history. 3. Interview people in school to learn about them and their jobs. Photograph them and show it as you report to others what you learned.

- MOBILE--Create mobiles for different textures, such as rough, smooth, and tough.

- PAINTING--1. Paint a rainbow, and explain its color sequence. 2. Paint a geometric figure, and paint dots inside. *I painted a _____ with _____ dots inside.*

- PHOTOGRAPH OR PHOTO SEQUENCE--1. Take digital photographs of items around school. Children describe a photo for others to identify. 2. Photograph a learning experience at school. Children place the photograph in sequence as they retell the task.

- POSTER--Create a poster using words and pictures to show others what you learned as you researched _____.

- RAP/SONG--Use the tune for common songs, such as "The Farmer and the Dell", to make up songs about math facts.

- REBUS STORY OR SENTENCE--Use stickers or small cutouts of pictures in place of nouns in a sentence. Begin with simple patterns. *I want a _____. The _____ can run.*

- RIDDLE OR RHYME--Create riddles for others to solve about the topic being studied or people in the class. *I am the tallest and oldest person in the class. Who am I?*

- SCAVENGER HUNT--Compute how many times a certain word appears on one page of the newspaper by highlighting that word each time you find it.

- WORDLESS BOOK--1. Tape record your version of a story for a wordless book. Place your tape and the book in the reading center for others to enjoy. 2. Dictate or write the words to accompany each page of a wordless book.

Kingore, B. (2002). <u>Rubrics and More!</u> Austin: Professional Associates Publishing.

PRODUCTS GRID FOR Learners with Limited Reading and Writing Skills

	MODALITIES					MULTIPLE INTELLIGENCES							
	V	O/A	W	K		L	L-M	N	S	M	B-K	Inter	Intra
acrostic	•		•			•	•	•	•			•	•
alphabet chart for a topic	•		•			•	•	•	•			•	•
audio tape		•				•	•	•		•		•	•
chart	•		•			•	•	•				•	
choral reading/readers theater	•	•	•			•	•	•		•		•	
collection collage	•			•			•	•	•		•	•	•
comic strip	•		•			•	•	•	•			•	•
concept or story map (web)	•		•			•	•	•	•			•	•
dance	•	•		•						•	•	•	•
demonstration	•	•	•	•		•	•	•	•	•	•	•	•
diorama	•			•			•	•	•		•	•	•
experiment	•			•			•	•	•		•	•	•
flannel board presentation	•	•		•		•	•	•	•		•	•	
graph	•		•			•	•	•				•	•
illustration	•						•	•	•			•	•
interview		•	•			•	•	•				•	
jigsaw puzzle	•			•			•	•	•		•	•	•
list			•			•	•	•				•	•
mobile	•			•			•	•	•		•	•	•
mural/banner	•			•		•	•	•	•		•	•	
museum exhibit/display	•		•	•		•	•	•	•		•	•	
oral report		•	•			•	•	•				•	•
painting	•			•					•	•		•	•
pantomime				•				•			•	•	•
photograph or photo sequence	•			•		•	•	•			•	•	•
picture dictionary/scrapbook	•		•			•	•	•	•			•	
picture book	•		•			•	•	•	•			•	
play/puppet show	•	•	•	•		•	•	•	•		•	•	
pop-up book	•	•	•	•		•	•	•	•		•	•	
poster	•		•	•		•	•	•	•		•	•	
rap/song		•		•		•				•	•	•	
rebus story or sentence	•		•			•	•	•	•			•	•
riddle or rhyme		•	•			•						•	•
role play	•	•	•			•					•	•	
scavenger hunt	•		•	•		•	•	•			•	•	
scrapbook	•	•	•			•			•		•	•	•
sculpture	•			•					•		•	•	•
wordless book	•								•			•	•

Kingore, B. (2002). Rubrics and More! Austin: Professional Associates Publishing.

Product Examples for Primary Grades

- ACROSTIC--1. Use a concept or topic word, such as **cooperation.** Brainstorm and write a significant word or phrase related to it that begins with each letter. 2. Use the title of a book the class is reading. Write events and details from the book for each letter in the title.
- ALPHABET BOOK--Write and illustrate an individual or group alphabet book showing what you have learned about the topic being studied.
- AUDIO TAPE--Record a book for the reading center. Make a sound for when to turn the page.
- COLLECTION COLLAGE--Work with others to create a collage for each color of the rainbow.
- COMIC STRIP--Draw a comic strip in which one or two characters tell how to do a simple process and sequence.
- CONCEPT STORY MAP (WEB)--Create symbols for characters, setting, problem, and solution. Use them to map a book you've read.
- FABLE--Write and illustrate a fable using your favorite animal as the character. Carefully plan your main idea as the moral of the story.
- INTERVIEW--Interview five people to determine how they feel about spiders and/or insects. Organize the results to share in class.
- INVITATION--Write an invitation to the principal or other school personnel to come to your room to read the stories your class has created or to view some other important work you completed.
- JOURNAL/DIARY/LEARNING LOG--Compare three entries in your journal. Tell one thing they show about you as a learner.
- LIST--With others, list all the words to say or write instead of simple, over-used words, such as **nice, said, good,** or **like.**
- MUSEUM EXHIBIT/DISPLAY--Create a three-dimensional museum exhibit showing what you've learned as you researched something that lives in the oceans. Make a card to display beside your exhibit that explains the most important information.
- PHOTOGRAPH OR PHOTO SEQUENCE--Use a digital or regular camera to take photographs of items around school. Write a description of your photograph. Ask others to read and then draw a picture of what you describe without seeing the photograph. Compare their drawing to your photograph, and discuss similarities and differences.
- POSTER--Make a poster called **Pairs** that shows different pairs of common things, such as: hands, eyes, button holes, and twins.
- REBUS STORY OR SENTENCE--Write a summary or retelling of the beginning, middle, and end of a book you read by drawing pictures to substitute for some nouns in your story.
- ROLE PLAY--Read Chrysanthemum by Kevin Henkes. With others, role play behaviors at school that would be **absolutely dreadful** and **absolutely perfect.**
- SCAVENGER HUNT--Create a scavenger hunt for words on a cereal box, such as: **find a word that means "good," find a word that rhymes with "cat,"** and **count how many items the word "in" is on the box.** Challenge others to complete your game.
- SCULPTURE--Make a paper sculpture using 19 sizes of paper and five geometric shapes.
- VENN DIAGRAM--Compare addition to subtraction, two dinosaurs, two characters, or two stories. Use illustrations for the Venn, such as a bow tie, a penguin with out-stretched wings, or outlines of two dinosaurs overlapping slightly to create three areas for writing.

Kingore, B. (2002). Rubrics and More! Austin: Professional Associates Publishing.

PRODUCTS GRID FOR Primary Grades

	MODALITIES				MULTIPLE INTELLIGENCES							
	V	O/A	W	K	L	L-M	N	S	M	B-K	Inter	Intra
acrostic	•		•		•	•	•	•			•	•
alphabet book for a topic	•		•		•	•	•	•			•	•
audio tape		•			•	•	•		•		•	•
book or booklet	•		•		•	•	•	•			•	•
chart	•		•		•	•	•	•			•	•
choral reading/readers theater	•	•	•		•				•		•	
collection collage	•		•	•			•	•		•	•	
comic strip	•		•				•	•			•	
concept or story map (web)	•		•		•	•	•	•			•	•
demonstration	•	•	•	•	•	•	•	•	•	•	•	•
diorama	•		•	•	•		•	•		•	•	•
experiment	•			•	•	•	•	•		•	•	•
fable		•	•		•	•	•	•			•	•
flannel board presentation	•	•		•	•	•	•	•		•	•	•
graph	•		•		•	•	•	•			•	•
illustration	•				•		•	•			•	•
interview		•	•		•	•			•		•	
invitation	•	•	•		•			•			•	•
jigsaw puzzle	•			•	•	•	•	•		•	•	
journal/diary/learning log			•		•	•	•					•
letter			•		•	•	•					•
list			•		•	•	•				•	•
mobile	•			•	•		•	•		•	•	•
mural/banner	•			•			•	•		•	•	•
museum exhibit/display	•		•	•	•		•	•		•	•	•
newspaper	•		•		•	•	•	•			•	•
oral report		•		•	•	•	•			•	•	•
painting	•			•			•	•		•	•	•
photograph or photo sequence	•			•			•	•	•	•	•	•
picture dictionary/scrapbook	•		•		•	•	•	•	•		•	•
play/puppet show	•	•	•	•	•	•	•			•	•	•
poem/bio poem		•	•		•	•	•	•	•		•	
pop-up book	•		•	•	•	•	•	•		•	•	•
poster	•		•	•	•	•	•	•		•	•	•
rap/performed rhyme/song		•		•	•				•	•	•	
rebus story or sentence	•		•		•	•	•	•			•	•
riddle or rhyme		•	•		•	•	•	•			•	•
role play	•	•		•	•					•	•	
scavenger hunt	•		•	•	•	•	•			•	•	
sculpture	•			•				•		•	•	•
story (with illustrations)	•	•	•		•	•	•	•			•	•
Venn diagram	•		•		•	•	•	•			•	•
wordless book	•							•			•	•

Kingore, B. (2002). <u>Rubrics and More!</u> Austin: Professional Associates Publishing.

Product Examples for Language Arts and Social Studies

- ACROSTIC--Use a concept or topic word, such as **Africa** or **Apache**. Students brainstorm and write a significant word, phrase, or sentence related to the topic that begins with each letter.

- ADVERTISEMENT/BROCHURE--1. Create an advertisement for an item used by a character or historical figure to solve a problem. Include how it was used and its current value. 2. Create an advertisement for a city or state you have studied. Use words and illustrations that will make others want to visit that area.

- ANALOGY/SIMILE/METAPHOR--Write direct analogies comparing a historical person or book character to a common object. **Martin Luther King, Jr. is like a broken clock because he ran out of time before he completed all the possibilities within him.**

- BULLETIN BOARD--Individuals or small groups of students make a bulletin board to highlight the publications and life of a favorite author who lived in or wrote about the time period or location being studied.

- CHORAL READING/READERS THEATER--Transform a classic fable, short story, or poem into a readers theater to perform for other classes.

- DEBATE--Debate the censorship of books in school libraries.

- EDITORIAL/ESSAY/PERSUASIVE WRITING--Write an essay persuading the school librarian to place in the library a copy of a new book you've read. Use supportive arguments explaining the book's literary merit and relevance to the student body.

- FAMILY TREE-- Interview family members, and develop a family tree that includes four or more generations. Surround your family tree with pictures and maps of where different family members were born.

- FLOW CHART--Draw and label a flow chart describing the sequence of events in a story the class is reading.

- INTERVIEW--Simulate an interview between a reporter and an famous explorer or writer.

- JOURNAL/DIARY/LEARNING LOG--Write journal entries for the main character of a novel, an explorer, or a historical figure.

- LETTER/E-MAIL--Write letters or e-mails between two main characters that discuss the book's main idea from their perspectives.

- MAGAZINE ARTICLE--Write an article about living in one city, state, or country. Take photographs, collect pictures, or draw illustrations to include in the article.

- NEWSPAPER--Create a newspaper for the historical event being studied. What is on the front page? What are the ads and sport events? What businesses need more help?

- PHOTO ESSAY--Read Russell Freedman's <u>Lincoln: A Photobiography</u>. Create a photobiography of the life in your community or a historical building in your city.

- POEM/DIAMANTE/BIO POEM--1. Create a bio poem for a historical figure or a character in a book. 2. Write a diamante revealing two diverse perspectives of Manifest Destiny.

- TIME LINE--Create a time line of dates significant to the social studies topic being studied. Challenge others to label your time line to test their understanding of the topic.

- TRAVELOGUE--Write a travelogue from the perspective of an early explorer as he pursues his travels and makes his most important discoveries.

- VENN DIAGRAM--Compare two countries by overlapping their outlines to create three areas for writing.

Kingore, B. (2002). <u>Rubrics and More!</u> Austin: Professional Associates Publishing.

PRODUCTS GRID FOR Language Arts and Social Studies

	MODALITIES				MULTIPLE INTELLIGENCES							
	V	O/A	W	K	L	L-M	N	S	M	B-K	Inter	Intra
acrostic	•		•		•	•		•			•	•
advertisement/brochure	•	•	•	•	•			•		•	•	•
analogy/simile/metaphor		•	•		•	•	•				•	•
audio tape		•			•	•			•		•	•
book or illustrated story	•		•		•	•		•			•	•
bulletin board	•		•	•	•			•		•	•	•
cartoon or caricature	•		•		•	•	•	•				•
center (student made)	•		•	•	•		•	•	•	•	•	•
choral reading/readers theater	•	•	•	•	•	•		•	•	•	•	
comic strip	•		•		•			•				•
concept or story map (web)	•		•		•	•	•	•			•	
debate		•	•		•						•	
demonstration (labeled artifacts)	•	•	•	•	•		•	•		•	•	
dialogue		•	•		•						•	
diorama	•		•	•	•		•	•		•	•	
documentary film	•	•	•	•	•	•	•	•	•	•	•	
editorial/essay/persuasive writing		•	•		•	•		•			•	
fable (illustrated)	•	•	•		•	•		•			•	
family tree	•	•	•		•		•	•			•	•
flannel board presentation	•	•		•	•		•	•		•	•	
flow chart	•		•		•	•	•	•			•	
game (original)	•	•	•	•	•		•	•		•	•	
interview		•	•		•	•					•	
jigsaw puzzle	•		•	•	•		•	•		•	•	•
journal/diary/learning log			•		•	•						•
letter/e-mail			•		•	•					•	•
magazine article			•		•	•					•	
map/salt map (with legend)	•		•	•	•		•	•			•	•
mobile	•		•	•	•		•	•			•	•
model	•		•	•	•		•	•			•	•
mural	•		•	•	•		•	•	•		•	•
museum exhibit	•		•	•	•		•	•			•	•
newscast/TV program	•	•	•	•	•	•	•	•	•		•	
newspaper	•		•		•	•	•	•			•	
oral report/persuasive speech		•	•	•	•	•		•			•	•
panel discussion		•			•	•					•	
pantomime	•			•			•	•		•		•
photo essay	•			•			•	•	•			•
play/puppet show (with music)	•	•	•	•	•	•		•	•	•	•	•
poem/diamante/bio poem	•	•	•		•	•		•	•			•
pop-up book	•		•	•	•	•	•	•			•	•
poster/chart	•		•		•		•	•			•	•
rap/performed rhyme/song		•		•	•	•		•	•	•		•
rebus story	•		•		•		•	•				•
reverse crossword puzzle	•		•		•		•	•	•		•	
role play	•		•	•	•			•			•	•
scavenger hunt	•		•	•	•		•	•		•	•	
simulation	•	•		•	•		•	•			•	•
survey (with data graphed)	•		•		•		•	•	•		•	•
symbols	•				•		•	•			•	•
time line	•		•		•	•	•	•			•	•
travelogue	•	•	•		•	•	•	•			•	•
Venn diagram	•		•		•	•	•	•			•	•

Kingore, B. (2002). Rubrics and More! Austin: Professional Associates Publishing.

Product Examples for Math

- ACROSTIC--Use a concept or topic word, such as **division** or **factorials.** Students brainstorm and write for each letter a significant word, phrase, or sentence related to the topic that begins with that letter.
- BIO POEM--Create a bio poem for **integer.**
- BULLETIN BOARD--Complete a bulletin board to demonstrate mathematical applications, such as: **Ways to Make 78** or **Examples of Geometry in Architecture.**
- CENTER (STUDENT MADE)--Use tangrams to create the ten digits and all the letters of the alphabet.
- CHILDREN'S STORY (ILLUSTRATED)--Write and illustrate a story to explain a math concept. As examples, read the three books by Cindy Neuschwander titled <u>Sir Cumference and the Great Knight of Angleland</u>, <u>Sir Cumference and the Dragon of Pi</u>, and <u>Sir Cumference and the First Round Table</u>.
- COLLAGE--Organize a collage showing fractions in daily life.
- CONTENT PUZZLES--Write key math facts on a simple outline. Cut it into puzzle pieces for others to put back together by correctly matching the problem and the solution.
- DEMONSTRATION--Use manipulatives to demonstrate multiplication to a younger student.
- ERROR ANALYSIS--Analyze a problem that is flawed. Write what is wrong and how to correct it.
- FLOW CHART--Draw and label a flow chart that illustrates how to apply a specific math strategy or geometric proof.
- GAME--Create a stock market game or math fact rodeo.
- LETTER (MATH PROCESS)--Complete one math problem. Then, write a letter to someone explaining step-by-step how you completed that problem.
- MATH TRACKS--Draw a long track on a paper. Write one number at the beginning of the track and another at the end. Starting at the first number, use any appropriate operations (as simple as addition or complex as algebra) to create a continuous equation that concludes with the number at the end of the track.
- METAPHOR OR SIMILE--Express a mathematical concept through a metaphor or simile, such as: **Addition is like compound words, and subtraction is like contractions.**
- NUMBER CHALLENGE--Set a challenge number for pairs of students to reach using dice and any appropriate math operations (as simple as addition or complex as algebra).
- QUESTIONNAIRE--Conduct a questionnaire asking adults how math is needed in their jobs, and graph the results.
- REVERSE CROSSWORD PUZZLE--Provide the completed puzzle grid of numbers. Others write the math facts that resulted in those numbers.
- RIDDLE--Develop simple or more complex riddles, such as: **I am an odd number larger than 6 and smaller than the square root of 81.**
- SCAVENGER HUNT--Provide a list of math terms to find in the real world.
- TEST (ORIGINAL)--Instead of taking a test, write the test items for the math process or concept of study.
- WRITTEN REPORT--1. Write a report about the real-life applications of a polygon. 2. Write a report regarding how and why different traffic and information signs are specific polygons. 3. Write a report relating how geometry applies to baseball or some other sport.

Kingore, B. (2002). <u>Rubrics and More!</u> Austin: Professional Associates Publishing.

PRODUCTS GRID FOR Math

	MODALITIES				MULTIPLE INTELLIGENCES							
	V	O/A	W	K	L	L-M	N	S	M	B-K	Inter	Intra
acrostic	•		•		•	•		•			•	•
bio poem			•		•	•					•	•
bulletin board	•		•	•	•	•	•	•		•	•	•
center (student made)	•	•	•	•	•			•	•	•	•	•
chart/poster	•		•		•	•		•			•	•
children's story (illustrated)	•		•		•						•	•
collage	•		•	•	•			•			•	•
content puzzles	•		•	•	•			•			•	
demonstration	•	•	•	•	•	•	•	•	•	•	•	•
diagram (labeled)	•		•		•	•	•				•	•
encyclopedia entry			•		•						•	•
error analysis	•		•		•						•	•
flow chart	•		•		•	•		•			•	•
game	•	•	•	•	•	•		•	•	•	•	•
glossary			•		•						•	•
graph	•		•		•		•	•			•	•
jigsaw puzzle	•			•		•		•		•	•	•
learning log			•		•							•
letter (math process)	•		•		•						•	•
list			•		•						•	
math tracks	•		•	•	•			•			•	•
metaphor or simile	•	•	•		•						•	•
model	•			•	•		•	•	•	•	•	•
number challenge	•	•	•		•	•		•			•	•
number line	•		•	•	•	•		•			•	•
oral report/informative speech	•	•	•	•	•	•					•	•
patterns	•		•	•	•	•		•	•		•	•
questionnaire (data graphed)		•	•		•	•					•	
rap		•		•	•				•	•	•	
recipe			•		•						•	•
reverse crossword puzzle	•		•		•			•			•	
riddle		•	•		•						•	
scavenger hunt	•		•	•	•					•	•	
song (original)		•	•		•	•			•		•	•
story problem (original)	•		•		•	•		•			•	•
survey (with data graphed)	•		•		•	•	•	•			•	
test (original)	•	•	•		•			•			•	•
time line	•		•		•	•		•			•	
Venn diagram	•		•		•	•		•			•	•
written report			•		•	•					•	•

Kingore, B. (2002). Rubrics and More! Austin: Professional Associates Publishing.

Product Examples for Science

- ACROSTIC--Use a concept or topic word such as **photosynthesis.** Students brainstorm and write for each letter a scientific word, phrase, or sentence related to the topic that begins with that letter.
- AUDIO TAPE--Record the sounds of a season or species for others to identify.
- BULLETIN BOARD--Compare and contrast states of matter or life forms in Antarctica with life in the Arctic Ocean.
- CENTER (STUDENT MADE)--Collect and categorize items that magnets do and do not attract.
- CHART/POSTER--Illustrate and label the physics principles demonstrated by amusement park attractions.
- CHORAL READING/READERS THEATER--Perform one or more of the choral readings about insects in <u>Joyful Noise: Poems for Two Voices</u> by Paul Fleischman. Use that format to organize and write facts about other animals or plants.
- COLLECTION COLLAGE--Use a digital camera to complete a collage of photographs of simple and complex machines found at home.
- CRITIQUE--Critique how the scientific method was applied during a specific experiment conducted in class.
- DEBATE--Debate the issues of using animals for research studies.
- ENCYCLOPEDIA ENTRY--Write and illustrate a ficticious encyclopedia entry about a newly discovered life form on another planet. Include specific information about its habitat, physicality, behavior, and life cycle.
- EXPERIMENT/DEMONSTRATION--Demonstrate how to use a piece of scientific equipment. It may be as simple as a magnet or complex as an electrocardiograph.
- FLOW CHART--Use a flow chart to demonstrate a life cycle, such as a butterfly or frog.
- GRAPH--Graph the weather in your area for one month. Compare it to a Farmer's Almanac 100 years earlier. Record three observations or conclusions.
- MOBILE--Make a mobile that represents the relationship of our solar system or galaxy to the latest discoveries in space.
- MODEL--Use common items as symbols to construct a DNA chain. Explain the reason for your symbols.
- POEM/DIAMANTE/BIO POEM--Write a diamante contrasting two opposite forces of nature.
- REVERSE CROSSWORD PUZZLE--Write science terms in the grid. Challenge others to write the descriptors that result in those terms.
- RIDDLE/RHYME--Create simple or more complex riddles using science concepts, such as: **I magnify things you can not see and focus them when you look through me.**
- SCAVENGER HUNT--Conduct a scavenger hunt of which ones and how many chemicals are found in your kitchen.
- TERRARIUM--Establish a terrarium, and write out the sequence of procedures you did to completed it.
- TIME LINE--Complete a time line and map of the progression of a major tropical storm. Compare your results with others in the class to interpret similarities.
- VENN DIAGRAM--1. Over-lap four circles to create a four-way Venn that compares the similarities and differences of four biomes. 2. Use a Venn diagram to compare the attributes of two species or the same species living in two different biomes.

Kingore, B. (2002). <u>Rubrics and More!</u> Austin: Professional Associates Publishing.

PRODUCTS GRID FOR Science

	MODALITIES				MULTIPLE INTELLIGENCES							
	V	O/A	W	K	L	L-M	N	S	M	B-K	Inter	Intra
acrostic	•		•		•	•	•	•			•	•
audio tape		•			•	•	•		•		•	•
book/booklet	•		•		•	•	•	•			•	•
bulletin board	•		•	•	•	•	•	•		•	•	•
center (student made)	•	•	•	•	•	•	•	•		•	•	•
chart/poster	•		•	•	•	•	•	•		•	•	•
choral reading/readers theater	•			•	•	•	•	•			•	•
collection collage	•			•	•	•	•	•			•	•
comic strip	•		•		•	•	•	•			•	•
concept or story map (web)	•		•		•	•	•	•			•	•
critique		•	•		•	•	•	•			•	•
cross section	•		•		•	•	•	•			•	•
debate		•	•		•	•	•	•			•	•
demonstration (labeled artifacts)	•	•	•	•	•	•	•	•	•		•	•
description		•	•		•	•	•	•			•	•
diagram (labeled)	•		•		•	•	•	•			•	•
documentary film/film strip	•	•	•	•	•	•	•	•	•	•	•	•
editorial/essay/persuasive writing		•	•		•	•	•				•	•
encyclopedia entry	•		•		•	•	•				•	•
essay			•		•	•						•
experiment/demonstration	•	•	•	•	•	•	•	•		•	•	•
flannel board presentation	•		•	•	•	•	•	•		•	•	•
flow chart	•		•		•	•	•	•			•	•
game (original)	•	•	•	•	•	•	•	•		•	•	•
glossary			•		•	•	•					•
graph	•		•		•	•	•	•			•	•
handbook	•		•		•	•	•	•			•	•
interview		•	•		•	•					•	
lab report with illustrations	•		•		•	•	•	•			•	•
learning log			•		•	•						•
letter (science process)			•		•	•	•					•
list			•		•	•						•
mobile	•			•	•	•	•	•		•	•	•
model	•			•	•	•	•	•		•	•	•
museum exhibit/labeled display	•		•	•	•	•	•	•		•	•	•
panel discussion		•			•	•	•				•	
patterns	•		•	•	•	•	•	•	•		•	•
photo essay/sequence	•			•		•	•	•		•	•	•
picture dictionary	•		•		•	•	•	•			•	•
poem/diamante/bio poem	•	•	•		•	•	•	•	•		•	•
rap/song (original)		•	•	•	•	•	•	•	•	•	•	•
rebus story	•		•		•	•	•	•			•	•
report (oral or written)		•	•		•	•	•	•			•	•
reverse crossword puzzle	•		•		•	•	•	•			•	•
riddle/rhyme	•	•	•		•	•	•		•		•	•
role play	•	•	•	•	•	•	•	•			•	•
scavenger hunt	•		•	•	•	•	•	•			•	•
scrapbook	•		•		•	•	•	•	•		•	•
survey (with data graphed)	•		•		•	•	•	•			•	
terrarium	•			•	•	•	•	•		•	•	•
time line	•		•		•	•	•	•			•	•
Venn diagram	•		•		•	•	•				•	•

Kingore, B. (2002). Rubrics and More! Austin: Professional Associates Publishing.

References

Freedman, R. (1987). <u>Lincoln: A Photobiography</u>. New York: Clarion.

Fleischman, P. (1988). <u>Joyful Noise: Poems for Two Voices</u>. New York: Harper & Row.

Henkes, K. (1992). <u>Chrysanthemum</u>. New York: Greenwillow.

Kingore, B. (1999). <u>Assessment: Time-Saving Procedures for Busy Teachers</u>, 2nd ed. Austin: Professional Associates Publishing.

Neuschwander, C. (2001). <u>Sir Cumference and the Great Knight of Angleland</u>. (1999). <u>Sir Cumference and the Dragon of Pi</u>. (1997). <u>Sir Cumference and the First Round Table</u>. Watertown, MA: Charlesbridge.

Popham, W. (1997, October). What's wrong--and what's right--with rubrics. <u>Educational Leadership</u>, 72-75.

Current Publications by *Bertie Kingore, Ph.D.*

Alphabetters: Thinking Adventures with the Alphabet (TASK CARDS)

Assessment: Time-Saving Procedures for Busy Teachers, 2nd ed.

Engaging Creative Thinking: Activities to Integrate Creative Problem Solving

Integrating Thinking: Practical Strategies & Activities to Encourage High-Level Responses

Just What I Need! Learning Experiences to Use on Multiple Days in Multiple Ways

Kingore Observation Inventory (KOI), 2nd. ed.

Literature Celebrations: Catalysts to High-Level Book Responses, 2nd. ed.

Portfolios: Enriching and Assessing All Students, Identifying the Gifted Grades K-6

TAKS Connections: Literature that Integrates TAAS Reading Objectives

Teaching Without Nonsense: Activities to Encourage High-Level Responses

We Care: Preschool and Kindergarten Curriculum for Ages 4-6, 2nd. ed.

FOR INFORMATION OR ORDERS CONTACT:

PROFESSIONAL ASSOCIATES PUBLISHING
PO Box 28056
Austin, Texas 78755-8056   TOLL FREE PHONE/FAX: 866-335-1460
www.ProfessionalAssociatesPublishing.com